AI-Powered Learning: Advancing K12 Education for the 21st Century

AI in K-12 Education

Adam Smith

Published by A. Smith Media, 2023.

While every precaution has been taken in the preparation of this book, the publisher assumes no responsibility for errors or omissions, or for damages resulting from the use of the information contained herein.

AI-POWERED LEARNING: ADVANCING K12 EDUCATION FOR THE 21ST CENTURY

First edition. May 31, 2023.

ISBN: 979-8223339533

Written by Adam Smith.

Also by Adam Smith

AI in K-12 Education

Intelligent Machines in the Classroom: Unlocking the Potential of AI in K12 Education

Exploring the Possibilities: A Guide to Artificial Intelligence in K-12 Education

Exploring the Possibilities: AI in K12 Education

Making Sense of AI in K12 Education: A Guide for Teachers, Administrators, and Parents

The Future of Learning: Artificial Intelligence in K12 Education

Towards an AI-Infused Revolution in K12 Education

Unleashing AI in the Classroom: Strategies for Implementing Intelligent Technologies in K-12 Education

Unleashing the Potential of Artificial Intelligence in K-12 Education: Reimagining How Learning Happens

AI-Powered Learning: Advancing K12 Education for the 21st Century

Breaking Down Bad Habits

Breaking Down Bad Habits: How to Overcome Self-Defeating Behaviors and Achieve Success

Standalone

Brain Dead: When It Comes To Improving Mental Health, What The Hell Are We Waiting For?

40 Things Intelligent People Do Daily

The Beginner's Guide to Quantum Computing & Mechanics

Open Source AI

Watch for more at https://books2read.com/adamsmith.

Table of Contents

Chapter 1: "Harnessing AI for Enhanced Personalized Learning in K12 Education."

Artificial Intelligence (AI) is the study of computer systems that act as though they have the ability to think and reason like a human being. It could drastically change our education system and make it more efficient. AI can help us by optimizing the learning process and by developing personalized lessons for each student, based on their individual needs. To harness AI for enhanced personalized learning in K12 education, it is important to consider several dimensions.

AI could help teachers identify a student's needs and recommend suitable personalized learning paths. AI-driven analytics can analyze the activities of each student, detect any learning gaps, and generate suitable individualized lesson plans. This could even help teachers and administrators to modify their teaching approach to suit each student's learning style. AI-driven systems can even record the frequency and extent of the skills students acquire or develop as they proceed through their course, allowing teachers, parents, and administrators insight into the students' progress.

AI can optimize the personalization process, allowing students to choose the subject they want to learn. AI can help detect which topics and subjects are most useful for a particular student based on their learning style, academic performance, and their interests. AI-driven systems can also recognize students' hidden talents and expertise and highlight these to teachers so that they can better develop and support instruction in these areas. In addition, AI could provide guidance and feedback to students for decision-making and help them understand their personal learning strategies.

AI could optimize patient record systems and timely diagnosis could be provided for each student's physical, mental, and emotional feedback. AI-driven systems could also monitor health conditions and provide automatic alerts when students show signs of illness or if they miss important tasks. This would ensure that the student can get the necessary treatment and support as soon as possible, improving their academic performance.

AI could revolutionize the assessment process as well. AI-driven systems could analyze the performance and identify patterns in student's answers to generate automated scoring reports for each assessment. This could provide teachers with more accurate and reliable assessment data that can be used to decide on the next step in a student's academic journey.

AI-driven systems could help reduce the burden of administrative tasks for school staff by automating record-keeping, scheduling, and communications. This could help free up time for teachers to focus more on improving instruction and student engagement, further enhancing learning outcomes.

Harnessing the power of AI for enhanced personalized learning in K12 education could revolutionize our education system. AI-driven systems could help with the various steps of the learning process, from assessment and recommendation to feedback and communication. By taking advantage of the advantages AI has to offer, educators can create personalized learning plans that can help students to reach their goals faster and more effectively.

Chapter 2: "Unlocking the Potential for Improved Student Outcomes: AI-Assisted Personalization of Learning for K12 Students"

The potential for artificial intelligence (AI) to personalize learning and improve student outcomes in K-12 schools is vast and exciting. AI has the potential to provide individualized, data-driven instruction that is tailored to a student's unique strengths and weaknesses. This technology can be used to help teachers identify and provide instruction that address specific student needs, provide automated feedback that is tailored to each student's performance, and provide students with real-time support in the classroom. By leveraging AI for personalization, educators can increase engagement, expand access to high-quality instruction, support all students regardless of their socio-economic or racial backgrounds, and provide deeper learning experiences for students.

AI-assisted personalization of learning has the potential to revolutionize how K-12 students learn. AI-based approaches to personalized learning are designed to integrate large amounts of educational data to create tailored learning plans for individual students. This process involves collecting information about a student's academic history, interests, and abilities to create an individualized learning plan that is tailored to the student's needs and interests. AI can be used to identify academic strengths and weaknesses and to prioritize the order in which students learn material. This data-driven approach can help students receive instruction that is more effective and targeted, leading to improved student outcomes.

AI-assisted personalization of learning also has the potential to support all students, regardless of their race, socio-economic status, or disabilities. AI-based approaches can facilitate individualized learning plans that are tailored to each student based on their unique abilities and needs. For example, AI can be used to identify which instructional materials are most appropriate for a student and provide feedback to the student in real-time. This approach has the potential to eliminate the need for traditional instruction methods, providing students with more constructive feedback that can help them learn faster. AI can also be used to support students with disabilities by facilitating the use of assistive technology and modifying instruction to provide accessible educational content.

AI-assisted personalization of learning can provide deeper and more engaging learning experiences for K-12 students. AI-based approaches can provide teachers and students with tools to customize learning based on a student's unique interests and abilities, allowing the student to learn more effectively. AI can also provide teachers with real-time data to support personalized instruction and to identify areas for additional instruction and support. This approach can also improve engagement by offering students a greater variety of instructional materials and activities to engage with.

Understanding student's data to improve learning outcomes is an area of education that is gradually being leveraged by K-12 educators. AI-assisted personalization of learning has the potential to revolutionize how K-12 students learn, and to improve student outcomes by providing more targeted and effective instruction for all students. AI-based approaches have the potential to eliminate the need for traditional instruction methods, providing students with the personalized learning experiences they need for to be successful. By leveraging AI-assisted personalization of learning, the K-12 education system can unlock the potential for improved student outcomes.

Chapter 3: "Unlocking the Potential of AI-Assisted Personalized Learning in K12 Education"

Artificial intelligence (AI)-assisted personalized learning (APL) has become one of the most promising approaches to increasing student learning outcomes in K-12 education. AI-assisted personalized learning is a learning style that uses AI technology and machine-learning algorithms to provide personalized instruction to each student based on their individual needs. The technology gives teachers access to data-driven insights that enable them to tailor their instruction and tailor their response to each student's learning behaviors.

In K-12 education, AI-assisted personalized learning has the potential to revolutionize how teachers deliver instruction. It can provide immediate and meaningful feedback to both teachers and students as they progress through the material. AI-assisted personalized learning can also help teachers anticipate and respond to individual student needs more effectively than ever before.

This technology can be used to offer personalized learning experiences both in the classroom and online. AI-assisted personalized learning technology can be used to track student progress and provide real-time feedback, personalized assignments and projects, and customized learning paths. AI-assisted personalized learning is also used to create engagement and motivation in the classroom, offering a more immersive experience to both students and teachers.

The potential benefits of AI-assisted personalized learning in K-12 education are numerous. AI-assisted personalized learning offers an increased level of personalization for each student. It can accommodate different student learning styles and preferences, offering support and challenges suited to each individual student. AI-assisted personalized learning also allows for improved student-teacher relationships as teachers can develop an understanding of each student's particular needs and learning styles over time. Additionally, AI-assisted personalized learning can help teachers and students save valuable time normally spent on administrative tasks such as grade tracking, allowing more time for learning.

Another key benefit of AI-assisted personalized learning is its ability to incorporate resources outside the classroom. Through its predictive analytics capabilities, AI-assisted technology can identify learning materials and resources that would work best for each student. AI-assisted personalized learning is also able to provide personalized instruction and help teachers and students take advantage of online resources. Moreover, AI-assisted personalized learning enables students to collaborate with peers and reach out to experts in their field, thereby expanding the scope of their learning.

AI-assisted personalized learning has the potential to provide enormous cost savings. By reducing the need for expensive instructional materials and offering more personalized instruction, AI-assisted personalized learning can help reduce the cost of running schools.

There is tremendous potential for AI-assisted personalized learning to revolutionize K-12 education. AI-assisted personalized learning can provide personalized instruction tailored to each student while also helping teachers and students save time and money. By harnessing the power of AI technology to offer personalized instruction and personalized learning paths, schools can ensure that each student receives the best instruction and support possible. In doing so, they can unlock the potential of AI-assisted personalized learning in K-12 education.

Chapter 4: "Harnessing AI to Enhance Learning Experiences for K12 Students."

As technology advances, it is becoming increasingly important for educators to find ways to use artificial intelligence (AI) to enhance learning experiences for students in their K12 classrooms. AI technologies enable educators to create more personalized learning experiences for their students, as well as provide better access to information and automated assistance. AI can also be used to facilitate collaborations among students, provide insights into student behavior, and offer suggestions for how to improve educational outcomes.

Classroom Learning

AI technologies can be used to personalize each student's learning experience. For example, AI can be used to tailor the curriculum to the student's individual needs and interests, allowing teachers to make sure materials are more engaging and relevant for their students. AI can also be used to provide timely feedback and assistance to both students and teachers alike. Automated grading systems, for instance, can allow teachers to quickly grade and provide feedback on student assignments while freeing up the teacher's time to spend more time with individual students. AI-assisted tutoring systems can offer personal and real-time tutoring to help students understand concepts and assignments.

Team Collaboration

AI can be used to enhance team collaborations and classroom discussions. AI 'social-bots' could provide students with assistance in understanding and constructing multiple perspectives within a discussion, focusing group dynamics on the content rather than interpersonal relationships. AI can also aid in formulating more cogent arguments and increasing the quality of engagement by helping students understand multiple perspectives.

Insights into Student Behavior

AI can be used to gather data on student behavior and engagement, so that teachers can better adapt their teaching methods. AI can be used to track interactions among students in the classroom, or keep track of how long students spend on certain tasks, allowing teachers to flag any activities that may be problematic and offer individualized support. AI-enabled systems can also help educators keep track of student performance and student engagement, offering important insights into how successful the current lesson plans are in motivating the students.

Suggestions for Improvement

AI technology can also offer suggestions for classroom instruction and student performance improvement. For example, AI-enabled systems can track student progress and provide teachers with actionable insights such as which topics may need more focus or where additional resources might be beneficial. Additionally, AI can be used to keep track of student successes to inspire and motivate them to keep striving for their learning goals.

AI technology is a powerful tool for providing K12 students with personalized and engaging learning experiences. AI enables teachers to provide tailored curricula and automated support to each student, as well as to facilitate team collaborations and gain insights into the effectiveness of their teaching methods. Moreover, AI can be used to provide data-driven suggestions for improvement that can help educators create the best teaching experience possible for their students. Through AI, teachers can ensure that their students have the best educational opportunities available to them.

Chapter 5: "A Perfect Blend of Artificial Intelligence and Personalized Learning: Leveraging AI to Enhance K12 Student Outcomes."

The promise of artificial intelligence (AI) is vast and its potential to revolutionize the educational landscape is immense. AI has the potential to revolutionize our current educational systems by providing personalized learning to students at all levels, from kindergarten through 12th grade. AI-based personalized learning platforms provide individualized assistance for each student, adjusting to their unique learning style and ability level.

For example, AI-based adaptive learning platforms can access huge amounts of data on each student, such as their interests, educational level, social and emotional factors, and preferences. This data can be used to suggest more appropriate learning objectives and provide the right type of instruction for each student's level of ability and background.

Another potential benefit of AI-based personalized learning for K-12 students is the ability to effectively "teach to the test." AI systems can analyze data from thousands of past student tests and provide real-time feedback and guidance to those students who are currently taking the test. For example, AI can provide guidance on how to read and understand questions, how to analyze data and infer connections, and how to select the best answer from a range of choices.

In addition to adaptive learning platforms and "teaching to the test", AI can be used to develop personalized plans for the entire school year. AI systems can analyze data from a wealth of sources, including student outcomes from past school years and current classroom performance. This data can be used to identify areas where students need additional assistance and target resources to those areas to ensure students are able to reach their full potential.

AI-based personalized learning can be used to assess student progress and provide individualized feedback. AI can track individual students' performance and provide personalized advice on how to improve areas where they may be struggling. AI can also monitor student responses to lessons and assignments to ensure that students are truly encountering the appropriate level of challenge and material.

AI-based personalized learning holds the potential to revolutionize the way K-12 students are taught and assessed. By leveraging the huge amounts of data available to educators and using AI to assess student progress, AI-based personalized learning offers an opportunity for educators to ensure that each and every student has access to material that is tailored to their learning style, level of ability, and interests. This would lead to higher educational outcomes for all students and could transform our current K-12 education system into one that is far more equitable and effective.

Chapter 6: "Leveraging AI to Enhance Personalized Learning Experiences in K12 Schools"

The world of education is undergoing rapid changes due to advances in technology, especially artificial intelligence (AI). AI technologies such as natural language processing, machine learning, robotics, and deep learning can be used to create personalized learning experiences for students at K12 schools. Coupled with a well-structured curriculum and teacher support, AI can help facilitate personalized learning experiences for each student in the classroom.

Personalized learning experiences are centered around individual student needs, promoting higher levels of engagement and motivation. By leveraging AI technologies, K12 schools can use data-driven insights to customize each student's learning plan, enabling them to receive content and lessons that are tailored to their individual learning styles and best practices.

One way AI can be used in K12 schools is through virtual learning platforms that can interpret student data, customize content, and recommend individualized next steps for students. These learning platforms can measure a student's mastery of a subject then provide them with the appropriate material to continue along the learning path. This eliminates the need for standardized tests as teachers can measure each student's progress through the learning platform.

Another way AI can be utilized in K12 schools is through adaptive and intelligent tutoring systems. Intelligent tutoring systems employ AI algorithms to detect the student's progress and comprehension of the material. These systems can then create an individualized learning plan based on their output. This helps the teacher identify which topics the student has already mastered, as well as which topics may require additional assistance.

AI can also be used to develop personalized learning experiences in the classroom. For example, AI-driven digital learning assistants can interact with students in the classroom and respond to student inquiries in real-time. This eliminates the need for teachers to constantly monitor classroom activities and enables them to focus on each student's individual needs.

Creating personalized learning experiences for each student with AI-driven technologies can also be used to create meaningful collaborations between teachers and students. By integrating AI into their classrooms, teachers can design individual study plans for students based on their personal learning styles. This can help foster deeper levels of engagement and collaboration between teachers and students.

AI technologies can have a profound impact on K12 schools. By leveraging AI technologies, teachers can create personalized learning experiences for each student and design meaningful interactions to help them optimize their learning journey. From virtual learning platforms to adaptive tutoring systems, AI can help create richer learning experiences for K12 students.

Chapter 7: "Maximizing Learning Outcomes Through AI-Assisted Personalization in K12 Education".

Learning personalization has been a highly sought practice in K-12 education, especially as the need for personalized learning experiences for students has been apparent in past decades. Artificial Intelligence (AI) has opened new avenues of opportunity when it comes to individualized instruction. AI-assisted personalization in K-12 education creates a much more dynamic learning environment and allows educators to provide tailored instruction and support for each student. This article will explore how AI-assisted personalization can maximize learning outcomes in K-12 education.

AI-assisted personalization utilizes current advancements in artificial intelligence to inform and shape curriculum and classroom practices. This form of instruction utilizes datasets of performance and progress to create individualized learning paths for each student based on their needs and capabilities. With the use of AI-assisted personalization, educators can more effectively determine which types of instruction are best suited for each student and can track the progress of each student and make more appropriate adjustments if necessary.

The use of AI-assisted personalization in K-12 education allows for more tailored instruction. Teachers are better able to understand the needs of each individual student and adjust their teaching methods to better accommodate them. AI-assisted personalization also provides students with access to more personalized feedback from their teachers, which encourages and promotes self-directed learning. This personalized feedback also allows teachers to create and assign learning tasks according to the individual's strengths and weaknesses to further enhance learning.

The use of AI-assisted personalization encourages critical thinking and creativity in students. When students are able to customize their learning experience and take control of their learning, they become more engaged in the process and develop the ability to think critically and creatively in order to solve problems. With personalized instruction, students are also better able to make meaningful connections between the concepts they are learning and how it relates to their everyday lives. This helps to ensure that students are learning the fundamentals while also gaining valuable application-based skills.

AI-assisted personalization in K-12 education helps to bridge the digital divide. Because of the personalized approach to instruction, students of varying levels of digital access are able to receive equivalent amounts of personalized instruction. By utilizing AI-assisted personalization, educators are able to provide learning experiences that are tailored to the individual student's needs, regardless of his or her access to technology or resources.

AI-assisted personalization in K-12 education has the potential to revolutionize the way students learn and engage with their education. By utilizing AI-assisted personalization, educators are able to create and assign individualized instruction that can help to diversify the learning experiences for each student. This form of learning personalization helps to foster independent and creative thinking, while also helping to bridge the digital divide and increase access to personalized instruction. AI-assisted personalization in K-12 education provides a ground-breaking opportunity to maximize learning outcomes for students of all backgrounds and capabilities.

Chapter 8: "Exploring the Possibilities of AI-Assisted Personalized Learning for K12 Students."

The possibilities of AI-assisted personalized learning in K12 education are numerous, and its potential to revolutionize the learning process is undeniable. AI-assisted personalized learning is an education model that focuses on individualized instruction and feedback driven by real-time data analysis. This innovative approach to learning harnesses the power of artificial intelligence to customize instruction in a way that best fits the needs of each student.

Personalized learning, whether augmented by AI or not, has been shown to be effective in helping students reach their full potential in a wide variety of subjects, from math and science to history and English. While personalizing the instruction to better meet students' needs results in more engaged and motivated students, AI-augmented personalized learning allows instructors to do more than simply customize lesson content. AI-assisted personalized learning offers real-time feedback, allowing teachers to optimize instruction in an efficient and effective manner.

At the core of AI-assisted personalized learning is the ability to collect and interpret data to inform the learning experience. AI-assisted instructional models make use of various data sources to better assess student performance and easier target areas for improvement.

Data collection usually involves two components, first, collecting raw data about the student's experience with the learning content, such as how long they interacted with each task and their performance. This data is then combined with additional data such as student's demographic information, (e.g. age, gender, socio-economic standing) and psychometric data (personality, interests, learning style). This amalgamated data is then used to assist educators in making decisions about a student's progress and educational plan.

Using this data, AI can suggest preemptive interventions and provide personalized instruction that is tailored to the particular student's needs. AI may even suggest learning paths or activities that can be taken to help the student understand difficult concepts and foster deeper engagement with the material.

AI is being used in the form of virtual agents and robots to increase the effectiveness of personalization. Virtual agents can provide personalized instruction based on student data and interactions, while robots are capable of helping to build on current understanding by providing physical manipulation and sensory feedback.

The range of possibilities offered by AI-assisted personalized learning techniques bodes well for K-12 students. Time-consuming, tedious tasks like personalizing instruction can be automated with AI-powered systems, freeing up teachers for more meaningful interactions with students. AI-assisted personalized learning can also help to bridge the social and economic gaps that exist between students, making learning more equitable and accessible to all.

AI-assisted personalized learning can have a tremendous impact on the K-12 educational process. By utilizing this technology in appropriate ways, educators can improve student engagement, foster deeper conceptual understanding, and empower students to reach their full potential. AI-assisted learning can open up a world of possibilities for K-12 students, and with the appropriate implementation, can truly revolutionize the educational landscape.

Chapter 9: "Unlocking the Power of AI-Assisted Personalization in K12 Education."

The advent of artificial intelligence (AI) in K12 education has brought with it new possibilities and applications that can improve teaching and learning experiences. AI-assisted personalization within K12 education holds the potential to be a game-changer for both educators and learners alike. AI-assisted personalization can provide custom, targeted learning experiences that allow educators to tailor educational materials and resources to meet the individual needs of each student. This form of personalization can help bridge the gap between individual student capabilities and the educational resources needed to optimize learning.

There are many potential benefits of AI-assisted personalization in K12 education, including increased engagement, better student outcomes, increased access to personalized learning opportunities, and more individualized support for students. AI-assisted personalization can be used to assess individual student capabilities, track student progress, and customize the learning materials to match their individual needs. This type of personalization can increase engagement in the learning process, reduce dropout rates, and ultimately lead to improved student outcomes.

AI-assisted personalization can also be used to create student-centered learning experiences. With AI-assisted personalization, students can engage in tailored learning experiences that focus on their individual skills, level of understanding, interest, and needs. This type of personalized, student-centered approach allows teachers to create learning activities that match the individual learning needs and goals of each student, leading to improved learning outcomes.

AI-assisted personalization can be used to provide students with access to personalized educational resources and materials that are not readily available in their physical environment. This means that students can access learning activities that they otherwise wouldn't have had access to due to physical or geographic limitations. AI-assisted personalization can open doors to a world of personalized learning opportunities that students might not have otherwise experienced.

AI-assisted personalization can provide students with more individualized support from educators. Teachers can use AI-assisted personalization to better understand student needs, tailor their approach to match those needs, and provide targeted instruction and support. This can lead to improved student outcomes and better on the whole educational outcomes for the school.

Clearly, AI-assisted personalization holds great potential for K12 education. This form of personalization can be used to provide students with access to personalized learning experiences, increase engagement in the learning process, open the door to new educational opportunities, and provide more individualized support from educators. AI-assisted personalization can be a valuable tool in K12 education as it can help educators create customized learning experiences that meet the individual needs of each student, leading to better educational outcomes for everyone involved.

Chapter 10: "Unlocking the Potential of AI for K12 Student Learning: Benefits of AI-Assisted Personalization"

Artificial Intelligence (AI) has the potential to revolutionize the way K12 students learn by providing more personalized, one-on-one instruction. AI-assisted personalization is a learning model that tailors instruction to each individual student's needs, interests, and levels of understanding. By utilizing Artificial Intelligence, educators can improve student learning outcomes while cutting down on administrative tasks. The benefits of AI-assisted personalization in the K12 classroom can be far-reaching, making it an attractive option for educators looking to maximize the potential of their students and keep classroom teaching dynamic and efficient.

The most obvious benefit of AI-assisted personalization in the K12 classroom is its ability to customize instruction to each individual student. AI-assisted personalization uses big data and adaptive learning technologies to assess individual student needs. This data can be used to create personalized learning plans and customized lesson plans for each student in the classroom. AI-assisted personalization also allows teachers to adjust learning plans on the fly, so that instruction can be adapted to suit the current needs of the class.

With AI-assisted personalization, educators can also get feedback on the quality of instruction and help students identify areas in which they need improvement. AI can monitor student progress and provide real-time feedback on student performance. This can be used for further personalization of instruction, but it can also be used by the teacher to better understand where their instruction needs improvement. This could mean fewer times that students are required to review course material, as AI can identify which material the student already knows and which topics need further study.

To improve student learning, AI-assisted personalization also has the potential to save teachers time in the classroom. AI can help automate administrative tasks that can be time-consuming and often tedious. For example, AI can be used to generate reports on student performance, create personalized learning plans, and schedule student tasks. This saves teachers time, allowing them to focus on the quality of instruction instead of the paperwork associated with teaching.

AI-assisted personalization in the K12 classroom can help promote a more inclusive learning environment. By providing personalized instruction, AI-assisted personalization can help meet the needs of all students in the classroom regardless of their background, experience, or learning level. This could lead to more equitable learning outcomes in the long run, which is essential for helping all students reach their full potential.

AI-assisted personalization has the potential to revolutionize the way K12 students learn by providing personalized, one-on-one instruction. The benefits of AI-assisted personalization in the K12 classroom include improved student learning outcomes, an automated administrative workload, and a more inclusive learning environment. As AI technology continues to develop, it is certain to become an increasingly important tool in helping K12 students unlock their potential.

Chapter 11: "Unlocking Personalized Learning with AI: A Blueprint for K12 Educators".

As technology continues to grow and evolve, K12 educators have the opportunity to leverage artificial intelligence and machine learning to facilitate personalized learning experiences in the classroom. The ability to offer personalized instruction to students can help students reach their full potential, as it allows the educator to customize learning experiences and materials to suit each student's individual strengths and needs. While incorporating AI into K12 education is still in its early stages, it has the potential to systematically unlock personalized learning for students.

By embracing and leveraging the power of AI, K12 educators can create unique learning pathways and experiences tailored to each student's interests, skillets, and learning styles. AI can be used to analyze data on student performance, and can provide educators with insights on how best to personalize instruction. For example, AI can scan through textbooks and educational materials to highlight the most relevant topics and passages for individual students. AI can also be used to generate personalized interactive activities and simulations, creating a wide range of learning experiences tailored to each student's skillet.

AI can be used to create virtual learning environments, delivering a unique learning experience with interactive audio, visual, and tactile elements tailored to the student's specific interests and needs. Teachers can also leverage AI to identify opportunities for differentiation, tracking and monitoring student progress over time and recommending resources and instruction approaches. AI can provide timely feedback to students and teachers, alerting them to areas where support is needed, and ensuring students have the opportunity to master skills and develop their understanding of the subject.

Beyond access to educational materials and interactive learning activities, AI can also enable students to engage in more personalized discussions and one-on-one interactions with teachers. AI can facilitate synchronous learning environments, where teachers can connect with each student virtually and guide them in real-time. AI can also be used to monitor student behavior, enabling teachers to intervene when necessary and provide personalized support through virtual conferencing systems.

As more schools introduce AI into classrooms, K12 educators must ensure that they are leveraging AI in responsible ways. Teachers must be trained on best practices for incorporating AI into the learning environment, and must understand the complexities of the data that AI is gathering. Furthermore, privacy and data regulation must be taken into consideration to ensure that student information is fully secure.

Leveraging AI to unlock personalized learning can help K12 educators create a pathway for each student to reach their full potential. By empowering educators to tailor learning experiences and materials to meet each student's individual needs, AI can facilitate a learning environment where individuals can achieve academic success. AI has the potential to revolutionize K12 education, and K12 educators must be prepared to embrace this technology and leverage it effectively in the classroom.

Chapter 12: "Unlocking the Potential of AI-Assisted Personalized Learning for K12 Students."

The potential of AI-assisted personalized learning for K12 students has been increasingly recognized by educators and education administrators. AI can put forth personalized assessments and instruction for students, allowing them to learn better and faster. In this chapter, we will explore the potential of AI-assisted personalized learning and how it can benefit K12 students.

First, let's define what is meant by AI-assisted personalized learning. This type of learning is achieved through the use of AI-driven tools to provide tailored instruction and assessment to students. AI helps in the generation of tailored individualized content for students at their own pace and level of understanding. AI also allows for adapting the content regarding student's interests. As such, AI-assisted personalized learning is designed to ensure that students receive engaging and customized educational experiences tailored to their individual preferences and needs.

AI-assisted personalized learning offers several advantages to K12 students. Firstly, students are provided with personalized learning that takes into account the student's interests, learning goals, and performance. AI-assisted personalized learning provides an individualized approach to nurturing students' intellectual growth. AI can be used to help gauge students' comprehension of content and then adjust instruction according to these results. AI can continuously identify areas for improvement and generate individualized learning paths for students. AI-assisted personalized learning also opens the door to more personalized and interactive learning experiences for students. With AI, education providers can create and customize curricula for each student, allowing each student to have the unique and personalized learning experience that best suits their needs and interests.

Another benefit provided by AI-assisted personalized learning is increased engagement. AI can be used to create instructional content that is tailored to students' interests and is linked to their real-world knowledge. This can help to engage students and boost their interest in subjects, resulting in more productive and efficient learning. AI can also make recommendations based on a student's preferences and past performance. This can lead to more effective and efficient learning by providing personalized instruction that is tailored to the individual student.

AI-assisted personalized learning also creates opportunities for effective collaboration and communication. AI can be used to facilitate communication among students and teachers, allowing for more efficient and effective exchange of ideas and feedback. AI can also support the creation and implementation of group projects, giving students the opportunity to work together on tasks and challenges. This encourages collaboration and interaction among students, as well as promoting the development of critical thinking and problem-solving skills.

Finally, AI-assisted personalized learning can also help to improve academic performance. AI-assisted personalized instruction and assessment can help to monitor student's performance and help to identify areas where an individual student may need additional help. AI-driven tools can be used to make personalized recommendations to teachers and parents about strategies to help improve student performance. AI-assisted personalized learning can also allow faster feedback to students, increasing the speed of learning and progress.

AI-assisted personalized learning has the potential to benefit K12 students by providing tailor-made instruction and assessment tailored to the interest and needs of students. AI-assisted personalized learning also allows for teaching and assessment to be more efficient and effective. Additionally, AI-assisted personalized learning can help to increase engagement, collaboration, and communication among students, as well as improve academic performance. As such, it is clear that AI-assisted personalized learning offers many potential advantages to K12 students.

Chapter 13: "Unlocking the Potential of AI-Assisted Personalized Learning for K12 Students"

Artificial intelligence is becoming an increasingly popular topic, especially with the proliferation of machine learning and the promising potential that it holds. Over the past few years, the potential of AI-assisted personalized learning for K12 students has become more apparent. This form of learning, which combines AI with adaptive learning, has shown a great degree of promise in its ability to effectively teach and direct students' learning.

The potential of AI assisted personalized learning lies in the fact that it can address the individual needs of each student. This is made possible through the use of algorithms that are specifically tailored to meet a student's individual educational needs. Through this type of personalized learning, AI algorithms can recommend relevant learning activities and materials as well as collaborate with students to support them in their learning. The AI algorithms can also track learning outcomes and progress to suggest and provide feedback on a student's performance.

The use of AI assisted personalized learning can open up a whole new world of opportunities for K12 students. For instance, it can provide access to tailored learning experiences and access to personalized courses and materials. AI can also help to facilitate engaging and effective learning experiences that can be tailored to the needs and interests of each student. Furthermore, AI can provide students with guided instruction and feedback which can help them to focus and stay motivated during their studies.

By being able to quickly and easily access and learn from personalized material and feedback, AI enabled personalized learning can help students to accelerate their progress and achieve greater success in their education. Furthermore, it can help to identify and address the individual needs of each student, allowing them to receive unique learning experiences. This type of AI-assisted personalized learning has the potential to dramatically improve the teaching experience, engaging students in a more personalized way while also increasing the access to and use of educational resources.

Another educational benefit that AI-assisted personalized learning can bring, it can also open up other opportunities such as increased collaboration among students and teachers, enhanced communication and feedback, and better access to resources. This type of learning can also give students the opportunity to engage in projects that spark their interest, allowing them to explore ideas and topics they are passionate about.

The potential for AI-assisted personalized learning for K12 students is clear. By leveraging AI to help tailor personalized educational materials, track progress, and provide personalized feedback, this type of learning can provide a more engaging and meaningful learning experience. Furthermore, AI-enabled personalized learning can help to open up new opportunities for collaboration, communication, and resource use. As the technology develops and more research is conducted into the potential benefits of AI-assisted personalized learning, it is likely that the educational opportunities and benefits that it has to offer will only increase.

Chapter 14: "Unlocking the Potential of AI-Assisted Personalized Learning for K12 Students".

Unlocking the potential of AI-assisted personalized learning for K12 students is a big undertaking. With the rise of technology and the increasing availability of artificial intelligence (AI) tools, there is a great need to find ways of taking advantage of these tools to facilitate better personalized learning. AI-assisted personalized learning has the potential to provide K12 students with a more tailored learning experience that caters to their individual needs, skills, and preferences. Through AI-assisted personalized learning, the student's personal learning experience is created and customized to support their different levels of understanding, with lessons that are adapted to their level of knowledge and comprehension.

In order to maximize the potential of AI-assisted personalized learning for K12 students, there are several key components that need to be taken into consideration. The first component is the use of data. AI-assisted personalized learning requires data to inform and refine the learning process. For example, data such as student responses to questions, engagement levels on assignments, and other sources of data can provide beneficial insights. Data is also essential to help customize the learning environment, curate content, and guide the selection of instructional strategies used.

The second component is the use of AI technology and the development of AI algorithms. The development of AI algorithms is essential to help analyze the data and use it to customize the personalized learning environment. AI algorithms can also be used to create individualized tasks, assessments, and projects for each student. The use of AI can also help to identify patterns, analyze trends, and inform the development of new strategies and approaches.

The third component is the integration of technology into the classroom. The use of technology such as virtual and augmented reality, intelligent tutoring systems, and adaptive learning tools can be used to reinforce learning and make it more interactive and engaging. Technology can also help to create a more personalized learning environment by providing personalized feedback and resources to support specific subject areas.

The fourth component is the use of mentors and coaches. The use of mentors and coaches can help to provide students with more personalized support and guidance which can further enhance their learning experience. Additionally, mentors and coaches can provide students with personalized advice and support, which can also help to increase student motivation.

Finally, the use of feedback and assessment are essential components of unlocking the potential of AI-assisted personalized learning. Regular feedback and assessment can provide valuable insights into student learning progress and areas for improvement. The use of feedback and assessment can also inform the development of individualized tasks and goals. Feedback and assessment tools can also help to create an environment of support and understanding between students and educators, which can further enhance the learning experience.

Unlocking the potential of AI-assisted personalized learning for K12 students is a process that requires careful analysis and consideration. By taking into account the components listed above, K12 institutions can begin to create more personalized learning experiences for their students that make use of the latest technology advancements and AI tools. This can create an environment where students can learn more effectively, gain the necessary skills, and reach their full potential.

Chapter 15: "Transforming K12 Education with AI-Assisted Personalized Learning".

AI-assisted personalized learning offers promising prospects for transforming K12 education. It is slowly becoming a growing trend, as it enables students to receive assistance and advice tailored to their individual needs. AI-assisted personalized learning is especially beneficial for K12 learners since it can help to address educational disparities, create engaging learning experiences, and improve student performance.

AI-assisted personalized learning can help to address educational disparities in K12 classrooms. For example, it can provide students with personalized learning paths that meet their individual needs. AI-assisted systems are capable of analyzing student data to recognize trends or patterns, and then suggest learning materials and activities appropriate for the student's ability level and academic performance. This type of personalized instruction can help close the achievement gap between students who come from different socio-economic backgrounds.

AI can also provide K12 students with engaging learning experiences. Through AI-assisted personalized learning, students can have access to immersive virtual interactions, personalized content, and engaging activities. AI-powered learning bots can converse with students and answer their questions, as well as provide targeted feedback to help them understand specific topics. AI-assisted personalized learning can also create a more engaging and personalized learning environment.

By utilizing AI-assisted personalized learning, K12 education also has the potential to improve student performance. AI systems can analyze student performance and give informative feedback to help guide students and promote learning. For example, AI-powered learning bots can provide context-sensitive remarks and ask students relevant follow-up questions to help them better understand and apply the material. AI-assisted personalized learning can also facilitate personalized learning pathways and assign tasks or activities appropriate for each student's ability level.

AI-assisted personalized learning offers numerous benefits for K12 education, such as addressing educational disparities, creating engaging learning experiences, and improving student performance. As more developers, educators, and administrators recognize the potential of AI-assisted personalized learning, its popularity will continue to rise in the K12 classroom setting.

Chapter 16: "Unlocking the Potential of AI-Assisted Personalized Learning for K12 Students"

Artificial intelligence (AI) has revolutionized numerous fields of study, with applications for education being one of the most prominent. As technology continues to rapidly evolve, AI-assisted personalized learning for K12 students has become increasingly popular in recent years. Personalized learning through AI can offer students a unique and customized learning experience, allowing them to explore subjects more autonomously and with greater understanding. In this chapter, we will discuss the potential for AI-assisted personalized learning and how it can be used to improve the educational experiences of K12 students.

Personalized learning through AI can be understood as the application of machine learning algorithms on students' educational data to personalize learning experiences on an individual level. This process involves the use of predictive analytics to model and predict how students can best learn a particular subject. AI can be used to identify gaps in student learning and develop personalized content accordingly. Additionally, AI can be used to assess a student's understanding of concepts and adapt material accordingly to ensure that the student is learning efficiently.

AI-assisted personalized learning also involves the use of intelligent tutors, which is an AI-driven technology designed to simulate in-person tutoring. Intelligent tutors use natural language processing algorithms to analyze student responses and provide feedback and guidance in real-time. These tutors can also be integrated with chatbots which can be used by students to ask questions, receive personalized recommendations, and get immediate feedback on their work.

The potential for AI-assisted personalized learning is immense for K12 students. Personalized learning helps to address the issue of the 'one-size-fits-all' approach to education, providing students with learning experiences which are tailored to their individual ability levels and preferences. This allows them to become more engaged in their learning, resulting in improved performance and academic outcomes. Additionally, AI can be used to track the student's progress and provide meaningful insights into their performance and understanding of the subject.

AI-assisted personalized learning also grants K12 students the freedom to learn at their own pace and in their own style, and offers flexibility of instruction. This type of learning also helps to bridge the digital divide, as it enables students to access personalized education regardless of their geographic or financial situations.

In order to maximize the potential of AI-assisted personalized learning for K12 students, schools and educators must take advantage of the emerging technologies and AI platforms available. This should involve using AI-driven insights to customize course materials and assessments, as well as integrating intelligent tutors and chatbots into the classroom. However, schools should also ensure that students are provided with human interaction in the form of mentors or teachers, to ensure that the personalized learning experience is as effective as possible.

AI-assisted personalized learning has a great potential to revolutionize K12 education. Not only does it provide students with a personalized and autonomous learning experience, but it also enables schools to better monitor the progress of individual students and identify gaps in performance. However, it is important that schools remain mindful of the implications of AI-assisted personalized learning, and ensure that proper measures are taken to promote ethical use of the technology.

Chapter 17: "Harnessing the Power of AI to Enable Personalized Learning for K12 Students".

The concept of personalized learning has been around since the 19th century but has only recently made significant advancements with the development of Artificial Intelligence (AI). AI technology has allowed personalized learning for K12 students to become increasingly efficient, cost-effective, and customizable. With so many advancements in personalized learning, it is essential for educators, administrators, and other stakeholders to understand how to maximize the potential of personalized learning in their classrooms and in K12 education as a whole.

AI technology has transformed the way personalized learning is delivered in K12 classrooms. Previously, personalized learning was labor-intensive and expensive. In order to give each student the individual attention they needed and deserved, teachers had to spend a great deal of time creating individualized lesson plans and assessments. This was not only time-consuming, but it also created excessive administrative workloads. AI has automated most of these tasks, allowing educators to provide more customized and effective instruction within a much shorter amount of time.

Another benefit of harnessing the power of AI is the ability to use data to inform personalized learning decisions. AI-enabled technologies are able to process large, complex data sets and metrics to provide educators with insights into student performance, learning styles, individual needs, and more. With access to this data, educators can personalize curriculum and instruction to suit the needs of various students, helping them learn more effectively and more quickly.

Specifically regarding data, AI-enabled technologies can also be used to make personal learning more engaging and enjoyable. AI technology can detect and respond to the behaviors of students in real-time, allowing teachers to better adjust their lessons to meet specific student needs. AI can also create adaptive, learner-based content—whether in the form of interactive applications or interactive websites—making lessons more interactive and interesting. It can also be used to create virtual classroom environments, enabling students who can't be in a physical classroom for various reasons to access the same specialized instruction.

In order to make the most of the power of AI, organizations should consider both the technical and non-technical elements of personalized learning. On the technical side, this includes properly deploying AI tools and utilizing data analytics to inform decision-making. On the non-technical side, organizations must ensure there are adequate supports for educators and administrators, who serve as the gatekeepers to personalized learning for K12 students. From training and professional development to helpful resources and access to community support, providing the necessary tools and resources to facilitate personalized learning helps ensure the success of AI-enabled initiatives.

As AI continues to evolve and evolve with it, the potential of harnessing the power of AI for personalized learning in K12 classrooms will only grow. With its ability to automate instructional tasks, collect and analyze data, and create adaptive, interactive content, AI has the potential to revolutionize the way we learn. By utilizing these tools in the right way and by providing the necessary resources and support, organizations can maximize the potential of AI and provide powerful personalized learning opportunities for K12 students.

Chapter 18: "Unlocking the Potential of AI-Assisted Personalized Learning in K12 Education"

The introduction of artificial intelligence (AI) into the realm of K12 education has opened up a world of opportunities for students, teachers, and administrators. AI-assisted personalized learning is a way in which technology can be used to provide students with tailored instruction that is tailored to their individual learning styles, interests, and needs. This type of learning can help improve student outcomes by providing personalized instruction that is available anytime and anywhere and that provides feedback that is specific to the individual student's needs. Furthermore, AI-assisted personalized learning can help maximize the success of teachers and administrators by allowing them to focus their energy on other important aspects of teaching, such as lesson planning, student engagement, and assessment of student performance.

To unlock the full potential of AI-assisted personalized learning in K12 education, many aspects of the learning process will need to be addressed. First, teachers and administrators must be trained in the use of AI technology and be able to effectively use this technology to create learning experiences that are tailored to individual student's needs. Additionally, data collection needs to be developed that can capture the necessary data needed to create personalized learning experiences. Another challenge is to properly integrate AI-assisted personalized learning into the classroom in a way that is seamlessly integrated into the existing learning environment. Lastly, appropriate resources need to be provided in order for students to be able to understand and utilize the AI-assisted personalized learning system effectively.

Once the necessary steps have been taken to ensure that K12 education can effectively make use of AI-assisted personalized learning, there are several advantages that can be gained. For students, AI-assisted personalized learning can help create customized learning experiences that will increase their engagement and improve their academic performance. Students will also benefit from feedback that is specific to their individual needs, enabling them to see the results of their work more quickly. For teachers, AI-assisted personalized learning can help lessen the burden of grading, thereby allowing them more time for lesson planning and engagement. Finally, administrators can use AI-assisted personalized learning to improve training and mentor programs, allowing them to make better use of limited staff resources.

The potential of AI-assisted personalized learning in K12 education cannot be overstated. However, in order to fully realize this potential, all stakeholders must work together to ensure that the necessary steps are taken to make this technology more widely available. Once the necessary steps have been taken to effectively integrate AI-assisted personalized learning into the classroom, students, teachers, and administrators will all benefit greatly by seeing improved academic outcomes, increased engagement in classrooms, and improved access to resources. The potential of AI-assisted personalized learning will surely become an important part of the educational landscape in the future.

Chapter 19: "Unlocking the Power of AI-Assisted Personalized Learning for K12 Students"

Artificial Intelligence (AI) has revolutionized the way education is viewed and delivered all over the world through its ability to create personalized learning experiences that cater to each student's individual needs and preferences. AI-assisted personalized learning is a process by which student-centric curriculums are developed which are based on the ability of AI algorithms to provide tailored educational material that meet a student's specific learning requirements. AI-assisted personalized learning offers a more affordable, efficient, and targeted educational experience while also creating a personalized learning environment where no two students have the same experience.

One of the key benefits of AI-assisted personalized learning is its potential to provide greater opportunities for K12 students. AI-assisted personalized learning systems can customize each student's educational experience based on their individual learning preferences and abilities. This allows students to be better prepared for their future studies and exams, while making learning more engaging and enjoyable. AI-assisted personalized learning offers students personalized instruction on topics they may not understand, as well as personalized feedback that can help them learn more effectively and quickly. AI-assisted personalized learning can also help students who have difficulty managing their own learning as it can provide personalized reminders and incentives to stay on track.

Offering more personalized instruction, AI-assisted personalized learning will allow greater access to knowledge. AI systems can provide students with access to a wide range of educational materials and resources that may not be available in a traditional school setting. AI-assisted personalized learning systems are also able to provide real-time feedback, which can help students better understand and retain the material as well as monitor their progress more effectively. Arguably, the biggest advantage of AI-assisted personalized learning is the cost-effectiveness for K12 schools. AI-assisted personalized learning systems can be deployed with little to no cost, which provides school administrators with a great resource for providing educational materials to students without breaking their budget.

However, there are also some drawbacks to AI-assisted personalized learning. AI systems are still not 100% reliable in providing the best educational experience for K12 students, as human educators still need to provide guidance and support to ensure students are mastering the material. Furthermore, some students may struggle with the personalized learning experience, as they may be overwhelmed by the amount of material or struggle with the individualized approach.

Despite these drawbacks, AI-assisted personalized learning continues to be a viable alternative to traditional educational models for K12 students. AI-assisted personalized learning offers a unique and effective opportunity for students to take control of their own educational path and achieve their academic goals. AI-assisted personalized learning also provides a cost-effective solution for school administrators that can help them manage their limited resources and offer students the best possible educational experience. Through AI-assisted personalized learning, K12 students can unlock their full potential and have access to a more engaging, meaningful, and individualized learning experience.

Chapter 20: "Unlocking New Possibilities: AI-Assisted Personalization of Learning for K12 Students"

AI-assisted personalization of learning for K12 Students is a topic that has generated much interest in recent years. Personalized learning allows students to tailor their educational experience to their own individual needs and preferences. Utilizes a digital platform with computer algorithms to customize a curriculum and pace of learning in order to accommodate the different learning styles of students, as well as their abilities and interests.

The application of artificial intelligence (AI) in areas like personalized learning can be seen as a major step forward in education, as it makes it easier for students to learn at their own pace and engage with the material at hand. AI has enabled the development of algorithms which can recognize both patterns and trends in data, and use these to ascertain comprehensive knowledge about a student's learning habits. With this newfound information, AI can offer personalized learning experiences for students that wouldn't otherwise be available.

It has been suggested that AI-assisted personalized learning can go far beyond helping students learn topics faster and more efficiently; it can also assist in helping them develop the skills and competencies needed for the future. AI-assisted personalization of learning in K12 will enable students to become independent and creative, as they engage with the material more deeply and collaborate with their peers.

Furthermore, applications of AI-assisted personalized learning provide a way to assess and measure the progress of a student over time. The information collected via AI can be used to create individualized progress reports and generate personalized instructional material. This way, instructors can better understand the needs of individual students, and students can work at their own pace within the framework of their own strengths and weaknesses.

AI-assisted personalized learning offers students more choice in their learning material, offering them the opportunity to explore new ideas, which can lead to positive educational outcomes. Courses can also be tailored to a student's unique interests, offering them the chance to explore their own hobbies or strengths practically. For example, if a student is particularly interested in physics, they can be provided with course material dedicated to that subject.

AI-assisted personalization of learning offers students more choice, flexibility and control over their learning environment. Students can become more engaged in their own education by having greater control over the material they learn, as well as having the opportunity to explore their interests. For educators, AI-assisted personalization of learning helps create a more positive and meaningful learning experience for both teachers and students. It is clear to see how AI can open up new possibilities for students in the K12 classroom, and the potential benefits are twofold.

Chapter 21: "Unlocking the Power of AI-Assisted Personalized Learning in K12 Education".

The increased accessibility of artificial intelligence (AI) technologies and applications allows educators to provide students with personalized learning experiences on an unprecedented scale. AI-assisted personalized learning is a growing trend in K12 education, allowing students to receive instruction and customization tailored to their particular needs. This trend brings with it many advantages, including providing an individualized learning experience, saving time, and reducing costs.

AI-assisted personalized learning begins with gathering data about each student. This data is used to create an individualized learning plan tailored to their needs, interests, and learning style. AI-assisted syllabi can identify material that the student may have difficulty understanding and adjust it accordingly. In addition, the data collected can be used to evaluate the student's progress over time and make adjustments as needed.

One of the primary advantages of AI-assisted personalized learning is improved engagement. Students receive lessons and resources that are tailored to their individual interests, allowing them to stay engaged and motivated in their studies. AI-assisted personalization also decreases the time and cost of instruction, as students no longer need to waste time on topics that are unimportant to them. By targeting areas of difficulty and weakness for each student, AI-assisted personalized learning can also increase mastery of important material.

AI-assisted personalized learning also has the potential to prepare students for future success. AI-assisted data can accurately predict a student's potential for college acceptance, as well as academic and professional success. AI can also identify jobs and career paths that best match a student's individual strengths and weaknesses.

In addition to its advantages, there are potential drawbacks associated with AI-assisted personalized learning. At the present, AI-assisted data sets are often incomplete or inaccurate. AI technologies are also limited in their capacity to recognize soft skills, such as communication, empathy, and problem-solving. Without access to sufficient AI data, educators must rely on manual assessments of students' skills and capabilities. Finally, some worry that AI-assisted personalized learning may lead to student data breaches and privacy concerns.

In spite of these potential drawbacks, AI-assisted personalized learning in K12 education holds significant potential. By personalizing instruction to meet specific student needs, AI-assisted personalized learning offers the opportunity to engage students more deeply in their studies, and help them develop essential skills and abilities that will prove invaluable as they navigate college admissions and career opportunities. As AI continues to evolve, its potential to unlock the power of personalized learning will undoubtedly increase.

Chapter 22: "Unlocking Potential: AI-Assisted Personalization to Enhance K12 Student Learning Experiences".

AI-Assisted Personalization to Enhance K12 Student Learning Experiences is quickly becoming a commonplace feature of the modern education system. With the use of AI, personalized learning experiences are now possible in K-12. Access to personalized instruction and support from AI-driven technology gives students the chance to build their own learning experiences tailored to their individual needs. This technology can be scaled up for entire classrooms and school districts and offers tremendous potential for success in student learning.

This personalized approach to instruction uses AI-driven algorithms to track individual student progress and performance. The data collected by algorithms such as facial recognition, voice recognition, and analysis of answers to questions can provide individualized instruction tailored to the student's specific areas of strength and need. This data is then used to customize the instruction and support they receive from teachers or other instructional aides.

An important benefit of AI assisted personalization is that individual students can progress at their own pace. AI algorithms are more effective at monitoring progress than traditional methods. They can detect when a student is struggling with a particular lesson or skill and adjust the lesson plan to help them better understand the material. AI-assisted personalization also allows teachers to focus more on individual students and adjust instruction to meet their specific needs.

AI-assisted personalization provides students with a more engaging learning environment. AI technology can allow students to interact with virtual assistants and learn in interactive, virtual classrooms. There is also evidence that AI-assisted personalization can improve motivation and engagement. For example, AI can generate personalized feedback and encouragement for individual students in response to their input.

AI technology can also make assessment more effective by adapting to students' individual learning needs and preferences. AI algorithms can provide faster and more accurate feedback and provide greater insights into student performance. This allows teachers and educators the opportunity to better track individual student progress and adjust instruction plans accordingly.

AI-assisted personalization provides significant potential to enhance learning experiences for K-12 students. With personalized instruction and support tailored to specific individual needs, student progress and engagement are likely to improve. With the right implementation, schools can use AI-assisted personalization to develop a more engaging and effective learning environment. This could significantly improve student learning experiences and educational outcomes.

Chapter 23: "Unlocking the Potential of AI-Assisted Personalized Learning for K12 Students."

Innovation in education has been increasingly growing in order to better equip students with the skills and knowledge they need for success in the 21st century world. One of the most promising recent developments in the field of educational technology has been the introduction of artificial intelligence (AI)-assisted personalized learning. This application of AI to education holds great potential in improving K12 student learning outcomes, but also faces several challenges such as cost and teacher readiness.

At its core, AI-assisted personalized learning is the use of technology and AI software to customize educational content and instruction for individual students. This can be achieved through a wide range of AI-driven systems, such as natural-language processing algorithms, neural networks, and machine learning. AI-assisted personalized learning has the potential to revolutionize the way K12 students learn by targeting specific areas of improvement through the use of AI-driven personalized learning plans. By having an individualized learning plan tailored to the specific needs of a student, educators can focus their efforts in areas where students need the most help rather than across the entire subject.

One of the most immediate benefits of utilizing AI-assisted personalized learning for K12 students is the potential for lowered costs. Using AI-driven learning plans can drastically reduce the amount of instructional time required per student as compared to in-person teaching methods. This could lead to cost savings for school districts, potentially freeing up resources for other essential educational funding. Additionally, AI-driven personalized learning plans could potentially allow students to move ahead at their own pace, allowing them to engage in more advanced coursework at the right pace for their individual learning needs.

Despite its potential benefits, AI-assisted personalized learning for K12 students is still a relatively new concept. As such, some teachers may be hesitant to change their practices in order to fully utilize the potential of AI-assisted personalized learning. To help teachers adapt to this new tech-driven learning environment, school districts should provide training and resources to get faculty up-to-speed on the effective utilization of AI-assisted personalized learning.

In addition to teacher readiness, privacy concerns have been a further major roadblock to the widespread adoption of AI-assisted personalized learning. AI-driven learning plans require a great deal of data, which could potentially open the door to potential privacy and security issues. To ensure student privacy is maintained, clear policies must be in place to govern the use of any collected student data.

The potential of AI-assisted personalized learning for K12 students is vast. When utilized effectively, AI-assisted personalized learning plans can reduce instructional costs, target areas of individualized student need, and provide a certain level of autonomy for students. To maximize the potential of this new technology, schools and teachers should take the time to become familiar with AI-assisted learning tools and strive to create a secure and privacy-focused environment. With the right steps taken, AI-assisted personalized learning could be a transformative force in K12 education.

Chapter 24: "Unlocking the Potential of AI-Assisted Personalized Learning in K12 Education."

In recent years, Artificial Intelligence (AI) has revolutionized the way modern-day education systems operate. AI has a multitude of applications in K-12 education, ranging from personalized learning and tailored instruction to automated grading and assessment. However, such solutions principally remain limited to discourse on their potential usage rather than fully harnessing the power of AI technologies to drive mass education as desired.

AI-assisted personalized learning (APL) has revolutionized the way in which student learning is administered and evaluated. APL leverages data-driven AI technologies to offer educators and learners a tailored, individualized learning experience. This provides real-time feedback on students' performance which can be used to inform, develop, and refine instruction. By using AI to facilitate personalized learning, educators are able to better monitor and support the development of individual learners.

The first step in realizing the full potential of APL in K-12 education is for educational institutions to take advantage of the ample resources and tools available. Institutions must ensure they are deploying the right hardware, software, and tools to run AI-based personalized learning systems. Additionally, AI-assisted learning should be adopted across all levels and types of educational institutions by leveraging existing learning management systems and inputting appropriate data sources. Each institution should also develop their own unique set of curricular objectives driven by AI-based personalized learning procedures.

Once this technological infrastructure is in place, AI-assisted personalized learning can provide educators and learners with virtually unlimited opportunities for growth. AI-informed instruction can identify inefficiencies within the instructional environment that can be addressed both efficiently and accurately, ultimately providing a more comprehensive learning experience for each student. For example, AI can detect if certain sets of topics or activities are not facilitating meaningful learning outcomes for a particular student. It can provide real-time feedback towards specific intervention techniques, enabling tailored curricula for each individual student and ensuring each learner is receiving instruction at the level appropriate for their specific learning needs.

AI-based personalization also holds the potential to further augment the learning experience through use of augmented reality (AR), virtual reality (VR), and similar technologies. AR and VR simulations can be used to provide learners with real-world situations they can interact with and obtain feedback on how they perform. Educators can focus on the specific learning outcomes of each scenario and utilize AI-driven trackers to understand the progress and development of each student in a more holistic manner.

At the heart of AI-assisted personalized learning systems lies its ability to build an interactive platform for both learners and educators. AI-assisted learning systems can provide multiple opportunities for interaction between the two parties and allow for more frequent dialogue and feedback sessions. It also enables collaboration, providing an environment where students can seek help from their peers. At a higher level, AI-driven systems also empower educators with better insights into how they can better design and alter instruction to better suit individual students' needs.

K-12 education is growing increasingly reliant on artificial intelligence-driven solutions. By leveraging AI-assisted personalized learning technologies, institutions and educators can realize a slew of unique benefits or their teaching and learning needs. Educators will be able to better enrich student learning through enabling customized and tailored curricula, while students will be presented with a range of opportunities to further their own individual progress. By unlocking the potential of AI-assisted personalized learning in K-12 education, schools will be able to maximize student engagement and further tailor their instruction towards getting the best out of their learners.

Chapter 25: "Harnessing AI for Personalized Learning Experiences in K12 Education"

Artificial intelligence (AI) has revolutionized the field of education over the past decade. A number of advances in technology have enabled educators to create personalized learning experiences for their students, allowing them to customize instruction and focus on student learning preferences and strengths. AI is continuing to show us more and more creative ways to harness the technology to benefit learners, and the field of K12 education is no exception.

This article will discuss how AI can be used to create personalized learning experiences for students in K12 education and why this approach is preferable. We'll discuss the potential benefits of harnessing AI for personalized learning, the challenges associated with AI for personalized learning, and the steps educators can take to get started.

Using AI for personalized learning experiences in K12 education can provide a number of advantages to students. One major benefit of this approach is that it can allow teachers to provide individualized instruction for each student. This means that they can focus on the student's strengths and weaknesses and tailor lessons to match their needs. This can also help to foster greater engagement, as students are being challenged in a comfortable learning environment that suits them. Furthermore, AI algorithms can help teachers to track student data and monitor progress much more closely, allowing them to make timely interventions when needed in order to guarantee that the student is succeeding. Finally, AI can also give students real-time feedback, enabling them to make instant corrections or ask questions about their work quickly and easily.

However, while AI provides a promising opportunity for personalized learning, it does come with certain challenges. One of the biggest challenges is that AI algorithms lack the sophistication of human judgment and can be limited in their interpretations. This can make it difficult for AI to pick up on more nuanced aspects of learning such as student motivation or the ability to solve problems. Furthermore, AI technology is still in the early stages of development and has not been fully optimized yet, which can make it difficult to create accurate models. Finally, AI can also run the risk of exacerbating existing biases, such as racial or gender disparities that can affect students' ability to learn.

Despite the challenges associated with AI for personalized learning, educators can still implement these strategies in the classroom. The first step is to familiarize yourself with the basics of AI and its potential applications in the classroom. Educators should look for programs that can capture student data points in order to create models, as well as programs that will provide real-time feedback to students. Once these tools have been identified, the focus should shift to creating a personalized learning system that meets the needs of each student. This may involve engaging students in conversations about their preferences, developing different pathways for different students, and customizing the learning experience for each individual.

By harnessing AI for personalized learning experiences in K12 education, educators can help their students to succeed. Personalized instruction can help to improve engagement and foster deeper learning, while real-time feedback from AI can help teachers to quickly and accurately track student progress. While AI still has its limitations, educators can take the necessary steps to implement these strategies and reap the rewards of a more individualized, tailored learning experience.

Chapter 26: "Unlocking Student Potential: Leveraging AI for Personalized K12 Learning Experiences"

With the advent of new technology, the education sector has seen a huge transformation. AI (Artificial Intelligence) now plays a crucial role towards improving personalized learning in the K-12 sector. AI-based learning offers a data-driven approach that enables students to learn in an interactive and personalized way.

Unlocking student potential by leveraging AI enables students to get the tutelage they need within the classroom or at home, using personalized learning tools. AI-based personalized learning helps match students and teachers with the most suitable content, allowing the teacher to focus on topics that students may need additional support with, or those that may challenge them to think beyond the given topic.

The implementation of AI-based learning does away with the traditional form of teaching. AI-based personalized learning is enabled by data-driven algorithms that can match students to the correct content, and offer them relevant activities. These algorithms understand the individual student's learning pace, style and preferences. By using AI-powered personalized learning, educators can better utilize their time in the classroom.

Data-driven tools like machine learning, natural language processing, and predictive analytics give K-12 educators access to student performance data, allowing them to better understand what students need. AI-based personalized learning can also help build meaningful relationships between students and teachers, creating an environment where teachers can really engage with their students.

AI also enables customized assessments for each student. By using AI-based learning, personalized assessments can be designed which take into account abilities, needs and preferences. For example, a student who is more of a visual learner might be better served with multimedia-based learning. AI-based personalized learning tools can also help teachers to gain better insights into how students learn. As students start to gain confidence in their knowledge, educators can use AI-driven learning to give them access to challenges and activities that may push them further.

Using AI-powered personalized learning also helps to develop students' soft skills, such as creativity, problem-solving and collaboration. AI-based learning environments create a more engaging and stimulating learning experience, encouraging students to ask questions, think out of the box and develop skills that may be vital for their future.

AI-based personalized learning can help to bridge the gap between rural and urban learning experiences. Students from rural communities often lack access to adequate technology, infrastructure and resources. Through AI-based personalized learning tools, students in such areas can access quality online learning without having to worry about access to resources.

AI-based personalized learning offers a powerful way of unlocking student potential in K-12. AI-based learning platforms are empowering educators to tailor learning experiences to the unique needs of each student, thereby helping them to get the support they need. Furthermore, AI-based learning is helping to bridge the gap between rural and urban learning, allowing all students to access quality learning experiences. Leveraging AI for personalized K-12 learning experiences is a move that educators should seriously consider in the ever-changing digital landscape.

Chapter 27: "Maximizing AI-Assisted Personalization to Enhance K12 Learning Experiences"

The use of Artificial Intelligence (AI)-assisted personalization has revolutionized the way students learn in K12 classrooms. It enables teachers to tailor individual instruction to each student's needs, interests, and learning styles. AI-assisted personalization has the potential to create more engaging and stimulating learning experiences that go beyond traditional paper and pencil practices.

For K12 educators, AI-assisted personalization presents a range of opportunities to enhance learning experiences. By leveraging AI and machine learning technologies, educators can create personalized learning pathways for each student, track student progress and engagement in real-time, and provide personalized feedback and rewards based on student performance. AI-assisted personalization helps to improve student outcomes by enabling students to work at their own pace and move through the material independently rather than relying on teacher-led instruction. As a result, students become more engaged and motivated in their learning, improving their on the whole academic performance and skills acquisition.

In order to maximize the effectiveness of AI-assisted personalization, K12 educators must be knowledgeable about the technology and be comfortable leveraging all available features. This includes knowing how to use the AI-based tools and software, and how to implement them in the classroom in order to effectively personalize learning. Educators should also be aware of the latest research and trends in AI-enhanced learning and keep an eye out for new products and technologies that may be useful.

Schools can also promote the use of AI-assisted learning experiences to students by providing workshops and seminars on how to use the tools and leveraging partnerships with technology companies to make the tools more accessible. Online resources and tutorials can also be helpful in helping students get started with AI-assisted learning.

District administrators must provide the resources and financial support necessary to implement AI-assisted learning solutions in the classroom. This includes providing adequate hardware and software, ensuring connectivity and cybersecurity measures, and providing teachers with professional development and training opportunities.

By utilizing AI-assisted personalization, K12 classrooms can become more equitable and engaging learning environments. For teachers, AI-assisted personalization provides a way to monitor student progress, provide timely interventions, and give feedback and rewards that are tailored to each student's needs. For students, it allows them to work at their own pace and move through the material with greater autonomy and control. With the proper support and resources, AI-assisted personalization can provide a powerful and beneficial learning experience for all students in K12 classrooms.

Chapter 28: "Unleashing the Power of AI for Personalized Learning in K12 Education".

The infusion of Artificial Intelligence (AI) into K12 education has opened up a world of personalized learning opportunities. By leveraging the latest advances in AI technology, personalized learning becomes possible for all students and enables them to learn at their own pace and on their own terms. This is particularly important for K12 education, where students come from a wide range of backgrounds and skill sets.

AI-driven personalized instruction enables teachers to tailor content and assessment to each individual student in a way that traditional teaching methods cannot. AI-based systems can continuously monitor performance and understand the individual student's needs and progress. This allows for timely and highly effective interventions and feedback. AI-based systems can also provide student-centric approaches such as adaptive learning and targeted remediation.

When combined with adaptive learning technologies, AI-driven personalized instruction can have a tremendous impact on student engagement. For example, teachers can create unique individualized learning paths and create digital resources that are tailored to the individual student's skills and interests. This allows teachers to maximize their resources and make sure that the most appropriate content and resources are being used to help each student progress and achieve their individual goals.

AI can also play an important role in helping teachers to gauge students' understanding and mastery of concepts and skills. By leveraging a range of AI-based tools, teachers can get detailed insights into individual student performance and progress. AI-powered analytics can also be used to identify areas of stagnation and weaknesses in student performance and assess how individual students are responding to specific teaching strategies. This enables teachers to take proactive steps to ensure the student is progressing in the right direction.

AI also has the potential to transform the way assessments are conducted in K12 education. By leveraging AI-powered assessment tools, teachers can develop unique and meaningful assessment strategies and meaningful formative and summative assessment tools. AI-driven assessment tools can help teachers identify areas of student struggle and, in turn, adjust classroom activities accordingly.

AI-driven technologies can also be leveraged to develop virtual and augmented reality applications that can be used to enhance the K12 learning experience. By creating engaging virtual environments, teachers can make learning more exciting and help students become more invested in their learning. Additionally, augmented reality can be used to create simulated classes where students can use their physical resources to develop dialogue and understanding.

AI has the potential to revolutionize K12 education and transformation in personalized learning and instruction. By leveraging the latest advances in AI technology, K12 education can be further enriched and provide opportunities for students to learn on their own terms. AI-driven personalized instruction could also help teachers to more effectively and flexibly engage with students and optimize their educational resources. This, in turn, could lead to improved student engagement, achievement, and ultimately, a better learning experience for all students.

Chapter 29: "Unlocking the Potential of AI-Enhanced Personalized Learning for K12 Students"

Artificial Intelligence (AI) has emerged as a powerful tool in the education tech field in recent years, providing educators and students with access to a variety of capabilities, such as course tracking, personalized learning pathways, and real-time assessments. AI-enhanced personalized learning presents great opportunities to enhance the effectiveness and efficiency of K12 education by tailoring instruction to individual students' particular needs and interests. This chapter will explore the potential of AI-enhanced personalized learning for K12 students, examining its potential benefits, its challenges, and suggestions to make it more effective and successful.

The most significant potential benefit of AI-enhanced personalized learning for K12 students is that it can greatly increase their engagement and motivation. AI technology can provide students with customized materials and activities that are optimized for their individual learning styles and preferences, allowing for individualized instruction that encourages students to become more self-directed and motivated learners. AI technology can also allow teachers to design experiences and activities that are tailored to their student's individual progress and needs, giving them access to up-to-date information and feedback on each student's performance.

AI-enhanced personalized learning also has the potential to improve student outcomes by offering personalized feedback and support. By using AI-driven prediction models to analyze data from past assessments and activities, teachers can better identify and respond to student progress and weaknesses. AI can also help teachers understand how students are responding to particular lessons and modify them accordingly. This can significantly reduce the amount of time and energy that teachers spend on repetitive tasks, allowing them to focus more resources and energy on improving student outcomes.

Despite these potential benefits, there are some challenges that must be addressed for AI-enhanced personalized learning to be successful in K12 settings. One of the most pressing challenges is the lack of reliable data on individual student performance. Without accurate and detailed data, AI models may not be able to generate accurate predictions or create personalized experiences. Additionally, there is the risk of bias and uneven distribution of resources and support. If AI-driven models rely too heavily on standardized tests or other factors that have the potential to be biased, students from certain backgrounds or regions could be at an unfair disadvantage.

To maximize the effectiveness of AI-enhanced personalized learning for K12 students, there are several areas that must be addressed. First, it is important to prioritize the collection and use of reliable student data. Accurate, up-to-date data is crucial for AI systems to generate meaningful predictions and insights. Secondly, schools must ensure that equity and fairness are taken into consideration when designing AI systems. This includes monitoring and addressing any potential biases in data and algorithms, as well as evaluating their impact on educational outcomes. Finally, it is important to use AI technology to improve instruction, not replace it. By augmenting teachers' skills and giving them access to detailed, real-time data on student performance, AI can have a powerful, positive impact on students.

AI-enhanced personalized learning has the potential to revolutionize K12 education by giving students and teachers access to a variety of capabilities that can greatly enhance engagement and motivation, as well as improve student outcomes. To ensure successful implementation of AI-enhanced personalized learning, schools must prioritize data collection, address any potential biases, and focus on using AI to supplement, rather than replace, instruction.

Chapter 30: "Harnessing AI for Enhanced Education: Personalizing K12 Learning with AI Support."

Artificial Intelligence (AI) is revolutionizing the textile industry and K-12 education initiatives with more personalized and targeted instruction as AI is adopted and deployed by educational institutions. AI has been an integral part of education since its inception, and its potential for future use is quickly being realized. AI has the capacity to play an important role in the personalized and adaptive learning process by delivering tailored instruction to individual students as well as personalized support to those who need additional assistance.

As technology develops and AI becomes more sophisticated, the possibilities for usage in K-12 education are really limitless. In particular, AI can be used to create a personalized learning approach which could produce better results than the traditional classroom model. The most obvious application is an AI-assisted personalized curriculum; this would provide a curriculum tailored to individual student's needs, taking into account their learning level and providing dynamic instruction to meet that particular need. For example, AI can create an adaptive learning platform which would monitor the student's progress and adjust the speed and difficulty level of the content presented accordingly.

Also, AI can provide personalized feedback on students' learning, allowing teachers to track individual progress in real time. AI algorithms and systems can provide personalized guidance on how to improve the learning process and pinpoint areas that need focus. With AI-enabled tracking, teachers would be able to provide more accurate and relevant teaching tips, strategies, and resources to help improve students' learning.

Adopting AI-powered systems would also enable technological advancements, such as automated grading and assessment capabilities. AI can be used to generate automated reports for staff and/or parents which provide detailed and timely updates on student progress. Moreover, AI-enabled systems can track student interaction online and in real-time. This data can be used to identify and address any possible issues students may be having with the course.

Integrating AI into K-12 education will also bring cost benefits for educational institutions, as many of the implementation and execution costs will be significantly reduced. AI-enabled personalized learning solutions require minimal human intervention, giving staff and teachers more time to focus on teaching and engaging in students. Additionally, the mobile and cloud-based nature of the system ensures that educational institutions can access the AI-based services and support anytime, anywhere without having to incur extra costs.

AI can play a major role in the collaboration process between students and teachers. AI-based systems can incorporate chatbots to facilitate digital conversations with students and provide timely suggestions and advice from the teacher's side. These AI-generated chatbots could also be used to track student attendance and provide automated notifications on absences.

AI is an invaluable resource for educational institutions looking to customize, personalize and improve the K-12 learning experience. As AI capability evolves, and technology develops, the potential to create personalized, and adaptive learning experiences will become even more powerful. The advancements being made in AI-assisted teaching, instruction, assessment and interventions hold immense promise for education, and educators must ensure that they are making full use of such potential.

Don't miss out!

Visit the website below and you can sign up to receive emails whenever Adam Smith publishes a new book. There's no charge and no obligation.

https://books2read.com/r/B-A-OSAW-KGVJC

BOOKS 2 READ

Connecting independent readers to independent writers.

Also by Adam Smith

AI in K-12 Education

Intelligent Machines in the Classroom: Unlocking the Potential of AI in K12 Education
Exploring the Possibilities: A Guide to Artificial Intelligence in K-12 Education
Exploring the Possibilities: AI in K12 Education
Making Sense of AI in K12 Education: A Guide for Teachers, Administrators, and Parents
The Future of Learning: Artificial Intelligence in K12 Education
Towards an AI-Infused Revolution in K12 Education
Unleashing AI in the Classroom: Strategies for Implementing Intelligent Technologies in K-12 Education
Unleashing the Potential of Artificial Intelligence in K-12 Education: Reimagining How Learning Happens
AI-Powered Learning: Advancing K12 Education for the 21st Century

Breaking Down Bad Habits

Breaking Down Bad Habits: How to Overcome Self-Defeating Behaviors and Achieve Success

Standalone

Brain Dead: When It Comes To Improving Mental Health, What The Hell Are We Waiting For?

40 Things Intelligent People Do Daily

The Beginner's Guide to Quantum Computing & Mechanics

Open Source AI

Watch for more at https://books2read.com/adamsmith.

About the Author

Adam Smith is a native North Texas Entrepreneur, AI educational expert, and educator who graduated from Embry Riddle University with a Bachelor of Science in Aerospace Studies. In 2007 he co-founded TeacherTube.com, an online education platform community that provides an educationally focused, safe venue for teachers, schools, and home learners. Under his leadership, in September of 2017, a publicly traded company, Salem Media Group, acquired TeacherTube.

After the acquisition, Adam continued his passion for technology and education by helping schools and start-ups to large corporations with digital consulting.

Read more at https://books2read.com/adamsmith.

About the Publisher

A. Smith Media is a fully integrated digital media and distribution company specializing in producing and marketing television, film, home entertainment, music, and interactive games. A. Smith Media has been at the forefront of the commercial growth of Digital Distribution and Internet Video on Demand services through its pioneering efforts in web TV.

www.ingramcontent.com/pod-product-compliance
Lightning Source LLC
LaVergne TN
LVHW022023200926
848481LV00007B/2518
* 9 7 9 8 2 2 3 3 3 9 5 3 3 *